Defective.

DHIRAAJ NAIDU

Contents

Originally published on Wattpad on 20th August 2019

Poem genre: Abusive relationships; Mental health

Written by Dhiraaj Naidu

Edited and beta-read by Farrzana Sheriff, Jasbir Kaur and Shannon Ng

Physical copies printed by Print City, Singapore

Formatted for digital with Kotobee Author

DJ Productions 2017 - 2019

<u>Intro</u>

3...

2...

1...

An old-timey clock chimes from a corner of the building. The signal reverberates throughout the old warehouse. Around me, all the employees look to one another, their eyes brimming with tears. Tears of joy. Tears of longing. Their faces screaming to their colleagues, their friends the statement we all knew around here.

Just like that, our last day here was done.

We were moving to a new facility upstate but wanted to work here one last time to soak in all the remaining strands of nostalgia we can salvage. And finally, it was done. We are finally moving on to a new place, to a brand-new environment. So, with one last look around of the whole place, all the employees said goodbye to the building, clocked out, and took the rest of the month off.

Well... *almost* everyone.

I was tasked to check every last room, to make sure the rest didn't leave anything behind and lock up. But I had other intentions. Once the last man left the place, I sped off to the huge storage unit. And first of all, 'huge' was a severe understatement. I'm talking lots of empty racks and shelves in a room so huge, you could stack a couple mammoths one of top of the other and *still* have room up top.

Awesome, isn't it? For most of us, it was a room of joyful memories. I know someone who met the love of his life in these walls. Someone was rumoured to have lost their virginity here too, being hidden away in stacks of crates and boxes. My point being, these walls were full of life, of stories, of laughter, of love. I am no exception, of course, but my memories here are much different than the average Joe. You see, I had my own secrets, my own past hidden away in a dark corner of these racks.

"Aisle 6... 7... 8. There we go," I softly muttered to myself as I entered the beckoning darkness. Turning on my phone flashlight, I kept walking on all the way to the end, my illuminated beam making sure to keep me on course. After a while of walking, I made it to what I was looking for. Sequestered in the back corner, almost unnoticeable was a medium-sized cardboard box. The corrugated edges were showing signs of aging, the sides were peeling away and tearing. On the top, the faded red ink almost made it hard to make out the word printed on the top.

-DEFECTIVE-

Brushing off the dust (and roach droppings) from the top, I set it down, opened the box, breathed a sigh of relief to find no pests in it and poured out all the contents onto the cold cement floor.

The contents were, as the label said, normal household objects, but either with errors in them, or broken. A sheet of paper with the margins at a weird angle; A birthday card with a typo so it said 'Happy Brithday!'; a heart locket with the hinge melted a little too strong; a perfume bottle with a crack on the glass… you get the idea. A lot of people tossed these items out because they were 'unusable'. But judging by the fact that I'm bringing this up, you could guess I don't see them that way.

And you'd be right. So, what if the printing is messed up? You could still use it to write! So what if the locket doesn't open? You could still wear it as a locket! As for the cracked bottle, you have *no* idea how much duct tape can help you.

So why do I collect these? Why do I collect broken things and lecture you about how they're not broken? Well, among those broken things was something else. This one wasn't necessarily broken, but it had been called such time and time again. It was a square piece of glossy photo paper. Stooping down, I picked it up and turned it over in the palm of my hand. It was a photo. A photo of someone who had been called 'useless', 'broken', 'waste' and so many other names. If I wrote them all down on this page. I don't think I can sell this book to teenagers anymore. Who is that screw-up, you ask?

It was me. I, just like everything else in this box, am defective.

Break Me More

Break me when I don't listen to you
Break me when I don't follow your orders
Break me when I'm not your dancing monkey
Break me when I be a human

Break me when I want some time alone
Break me when I need to heal
Break me when I'm not in the mood to listen
Break me when I break down and cry

Break me when I can't trust you
Break me when I don't tell you my cracks
Break me when you have to tug at the bandages
Break me when I pull back tighter

Break me when I tap you like you swing at me
Break me when I use your own cards against you
Break me when you have nothing else to say
Break me, because you can't talk normally

Break me when I tell you to stop
Break me when I can't take your blows
Break me when I push you away
Break me more when I tell you I'm broken

Your Fault

A hand you extended
A person you befriended
A loneliness you ended

It's not your fault...

Arguments you flared
Making us scared
then the damage you repaired

It isn't your fault...

Dividing us in two
Battle-lines you drew
Losses we couldn't undo

That's not your fault...

Driving us insane
Smiles we could not regain
Your marks leaving blood stains

That's not your fault... right?

Leaving us with heartache
Our minds you break
Biting us like a snake

Is that your fault?

Away you stayed
from a war you hand-made
A vow you betrayed

It's all your fault...

<u>Reminder</u>

You remind me
of all my worst flaws
You remind me of all the marks
left on me from your claws

You're a reminder of how
under you, my life was hell
You remind me of my old darkness
buried deep in a well

You're a reminder that everything
I own is all from your action
You remind me that love
is nothing but a transaction

You remind me of how
out of my grasp things like respect and control are.
Your reminders keep whispering to me
your casual remarks leave deep scars.

You remind me that you would
not care if I was dead
You're a reminder that my whole life
has no meaning, enough said

<u>Why?</u>

Why don't you get it?
Why can't you see?
Why can't you ever
understand me for me?

To you, I'm acting.
To you, I'm just dumb,
Are you that blind,
or are you just numb?

I hate explaining
I hate talking to you
You rearrange the pieces for convenience
dissing me as untrue

My suffering is nothing
to you who care about "only study".
I wonder when you walk in
and see my arms bloody...

Would you help?
Would you yell?
Or would you leave me to die?
"He's useless, let him burn in hell."

I tried to die
because you fail to see.
To you, my pain,
it's all idiocy.

You try to drown me,
but you don't let me die.
So in this empty void of suffering,
I sit alone and cry.

You've lost your child,
and you'll never get him back.
You now have a ghost.
Heart broken and black.

You can't help him.
He won't ask you for it too.
Because he's so broken,
your ignorance you can't undo.

Cruel One

You don't listen to what I say
My logic, you brush it away
My wounds, you leave undone
And yet I'm the cruel one

You never take my word
You favour the other one, it's absurd
I'm made to face the barrel of the gun
…and yet I'm the cruel one

I burn in your injustice like it's the sun
yet I'm the cruel one?
They push me to the edge, and you push me off
I am the cruel one?

I'm the cruel one
I'm the cruel one

I'm
The
Cruel one?

Well then…

I don't care about anything anymore
I won't even try
The person you call the 'cruel one'
Is the cold one now

To your lies? Cold
Cold to your injustice too
Because even when it isn't true
you name me after you

<u>Never There</u>

You leave me alone
and say you're too busy
to listen to me share.

But now you're mad
mad that I shut myself off
because you were never there

You always rush
rush to work
rush to make food
rush to buy groceries

All around me, you keep rushing around

And now you're mad
that I want to slow down
mad because you are never there

I turn to friends
to loved ones
to my therapist
to anyone

Anyone who can listen
Anyone who can understand
Anyone who can calm me down

Anyone who's there for me

Because I word the fact, you cry
You cry as I accuse you of being "never there"
Well, it's not like we can
and it's not like you try.

Sweet Dreams

Every night it's
always the same
Every night it's
always… him

I could still feel them…

His arms
around my throat
My eyes
welling up with tears
His legs
pressing at my femur
My lips
begging him to stop
His fingers
clawing at my hair
My ears
ringing from the blows landing
His silky smooth voice
nothing but insults and degradation

I wake up screaming,
wondering "can I ever sleep again?"
Knowing he's right outside my door
Can I ever be safe again?

When I fall asleep to
his voice whispering "sweet dreams"
I know those dreams
are anything but sweet

This cycle of hurt and control
I hate it but can't leave because
I still love him
and he does still love me… right?

<u>Badges</u>

I wear a badge every day
when I wake up
It has one word
in block letters: '**BURDEN**'

I wear another badge every day
When I sit in the lecture halls
It also has one word:
'***FAILURE***', bold and italic

My collar has another badge
Which I wear as a wedding ring
'**WORTHLESS**' it says, and
everyone can see it

More and more badges
are attracted so magnetically
I raise my arms and keep
letting them come and cover me

They are my jumpsuit
to protect me from the world
The badges with sharp blades
Make me not feel any pain anymore

I keep wearing badges
Because those stick like glue
People keep calling me that
So I follow too

I'm covered in head to toe
With all these badges
Now I don't even know
Under all these badges, who am I?

Interval

Tears run down my face, hitting the floor with satisfying *plink*s.

I apologise for starting this chapter off with something bleak, but most of the time, all these memories run like a sub-machine gun through my head; in rapid succession, and with each one wounding me with lasting damage. As light-hearted as I want the story segment to be, I also want to be genuine and honest with you.

Parents. Teachers. Schoolmates. Friends.

All of them had taken swings at my psyche, damaging it so much in the long-run. Now every time someone calls me useless, I find it so much easier to stick that like another label on my forehead. No matter how many times I try to argue back that I'm more than what that mark says, they would always look at the writing. 'Useless. Good-for-nothing. Loser.'

That label meant everything to me after that. Since no one wanted to listen to me, I turned that label into a badge of honour.

I am useless. I am a loser. I am defective.

Throughout the next few years of my life, I repeated that like a mantra.

I am useless. I am a loser. I am defective.

Again and again.

I am useless-

It became a thing I said to the mirror every morning.

I am a loser-

It became something I would agree on every time someone told me that.

I am defective.

It had become part of me.

It **is** me.

I was in such a rut back then. Looking down at the contents of that box, I chuckled slightly at how messed up my mind was. Mainly it was because of all of these external factors that I started to believe it.

You know the Mandela effect, right? You know, the whole thing of something which is complete nonsense being considered true if enough people say it? Yeah, it had happened to me for a fair bit. But fear not, I have moved on. But not entirely.

Looking down at the box, I knew that. I had to *really* move on.

Setting the box down, I jumped on it hard. The old cardboard flattened like a piece of dough. Pretty soon, the box I knew was nothing but a flat surface. And what do you do on a flat surface?

Picking up the broken mementos from my past, I stacked them haphazardly into a messy tower on top of the flattened box. Then I looked around the aisle. There had to be something here....

"Aha! Found it!" I yelled jubilantly, almost forgetting I was alone. I jumped at the echo of my own voice through the whole empty room in such a satisfying way. Lifting the canister in my hands, I tipped it over the pile.

Viscous kerosene oozed out onto the pile of reminders, pooling over around my feet too. Rummaging around in my jacket pockets, I found something else important: my lighter.

After a few rounds of flicking it, the flame lit up, its dim light further illuminating my little bonfire setup. Holding it with my left hand, I raised my right hand up toward the flame. In it was my old photo.

Mindless Haikus

Switch on, eyes open
Look outside, the sky's so blue
Thus the day begins

Sit down for breakfast
Simple meal, quick! Eat it all!
Now walk out the door

Absorb all lessons
Write notes, worksheets, nothing more
Now work with your kind

Try to talk to girls
Think of flat cute things to say
Rejection follows

Look out the window
Straight line traffic, simple minds
All these mindless drones

Dreams, hopes, fears, feelings
Nothing's real, here's your pay check
Go buy happiness

Do you feel something?
Glitchy system, you're broken
Time to turn

       you

   off-

<u>Medicate</u>

They say the pills
would help me
They say those pills
would cure my issues

Swallow them all up
Take as much time
for them to work
for them to fix me

Bright goes the world
Better goes my life
Thumps on the back
a clear contrast to my strife

And as the effects ebb
The world gets worse
The reality resurfaces
and they turn too terse

Can't live like this
Can't live like this!
To the nearest store I run
Those 'happy pills' I cop

I self-medicate
to again be joyful
I self-medicate
to never feel alone

Need stronger pills
Must. Feel. Good.
Move from the floux
to the heroin and cocaine

Now 5 years later
surrounded by my happiness
I still self-medicate
to break myself even more

<u>Back for More</u>

You hurt me so much
for so long
You kept me alone
in your 'safe' hands

I cut you out
and I'm finally safe,
so why do I want you
back in my life?

Why do I want you
to ruin my life again?
Why do I crave you
to break me again?

Your words like poison
But I keep wanting more
Your company a pain
But I still want to keep you around

Is it that familiar stabbing pain
like a blade biting into my flesh
that I get numb, to the point that
it's welcoming now?

Or is it the lack of any balm
anywhere around me, making
your backstabbing all the more brutal,
all the more damaging?

So many stab wounds, so many claw marks
they paint my back like a morbid mosaic
I pushed you away to let them heal
and to let myself understand what love is

Now I'm back for more
break me like you used to
Rip my self-esteem to bits
Tear me apart, because I...

Have missed it

Play Your Part

Lights on
Camera rolling
Mic'd up
Time to act

You put on your mask
And step out into the set
Another dull scene
Where you have to act

From the script given to you
with actors also wearing masks
to hide their tired and bleary eyes
and to keep playing the role

Their masks wear bright smiles
and dazzling dispositions
but their occupants are so honestly opposite
with so much pain, so much muffled thought

They fear to go out of line
For their co-stars would turn
Glare at you in both
annoyance and indignation

"You're wrong." "No one cares."
"Your mouth should only open to read the lines."
And if you cry, oh no…
That mask would slip away.

And the world would see…
Your 'ugly eyebags'
Your 'gross freckles'
Your- your-

The world would just see *you*
Without the mask or makeup
With all your scars, all your cracks
in au natural, out there in the open

Your fellows keep bugging you with queries
about your scars, why are you crying
Their curiosity and judgement seep into you,
breaking you even more from the inside

You scramble to put the mask on
and laugh whatever they saw off
And just like that, they turn back with
occasional pats for "staying in character"

You take a deep breath
and smile to the camera
Eyes blinded by the bright lights
and from your own tears

Devoid

I wake up
on a bridge above it all
Watching the world fly by
Waiting for that one phone call

Night sky, cold winter
Light shower, cloudy fog
Everything feels so serene
Everything feels so cold

Can't hear any voices
Heart rattles softly in its cage
World zooms by too fast
and then I'm plunged into darkness

I wake up in a black box
invisible walls, cold, dark
I bang at those hollow walls
No use, as I sink deeper into the void

Devoid of joy
Devoid of love
Devoid of fun
Devoid of anything

What is this? Someone I love calls my phone
"Hey, you ok? What's on your mind?"
With glassy eyes and sunken heart I reply
"...yeah, I'm fine."

Stay Out

I slam the door
and hold it shut.
On the other side
I hear your usual insults: a fool, a nut.

You kick the door down
forcing your way again.
Does it kill you to leave me alone
every now and then?

You finally push your way in
and find me – broken and on the floor.
Instead of helping
you destroy me even more.

I yelp out in agony
in pain, for you to stop.
But you? You don't.
You keep kicking me till I drop.

I drop to my knees.
and finally scream,
"Stay out!" as I shove you out
ending your cruel regime.

You roar through the other side
Calling me names, guilting me.
But you never help me, so
stay out; leave me be.

Defective

I take a swing at my soul
From my own lips, bleeding words are spoken
I punch myself till I bleed and bruise
Broken am I

I snatch my own joy
I don't feel deserving
I reflect toxicity instead
Self-loathing am I

At the edge I sit
But fear the deep end
Not wanting to hurt people I care about
I don't want a friend

Every second on this earth
I feel less and less like I matter
I often gaze out the window, thinking
"How better would it be if I were to shatter?

The idea of looking at my scars
makes me so hypertensive
So I keep hiding it to never think about them
Defensive am I

So many cracks and shards under my shirt
Hiding them is my primary directive
I introduce myself, but not the way I want to –
"Defective am I."

Had Enough

When I wake up, when I fall asleep
Every minute of every damn day
Rain or shine, even when the world's ending
You never shut up

Like a little imp you're there,
On my shoulder, shoving those
god-awful things into my head
Embracing me with your darkness

"You're useless." "You're a waste."
"You're undeserving of-" Yeah, I get it.
I'm a piece of shit, but I don't
need YOU to keep telling me that

Droning on over and over
about my shortcomings, you make me
lose any meanings and grasp on
what light even is anymore.

So help me, if you were flammable,
I'd take a torch to light
you up. Maybe that way
I would get you off my shoulder

Walk over your ignited, melting body
to scream in that cold, uninviting face
with a can of kerosene to dispel
your enveloped blackness away

"Yell at me, guilt me
Make a fool out of me.
I've had enough of your bullshit that
frankly, I just give no fucks anymore."

<u>Outro</u>

The warm glow of the flames lit up the room, as all the items were engulfed in the fire. Sitting atop my rudimentary bonfire was the picture of me smiling, its glassy fake eyes staring back at me.

Everything that was broken.

All burnt. All gone.

Even me.

As I sat taking in the crisp heat of the fire, I heaved a sigh of relief, using the light to look at my hands and arms. Yes, there were scars which built up over the years. And yes, those scars are there to stay. But they take a while to heal. They always will. What makes you defective, broken, a failure, a worthless nobody – those will always be there.

What you do with them varies from person to person, but eventually you have to accept that we're all broken and defective inside, and move forward. As soon as those items finished burning to a crisp, I got up. Taking one last look at the charred box with remnants of all those broken things, I smiled.

"Goodbye," I whispered as I walked out the door, locking it. I needed to give those keys back. As I stepped outside the old warehouse and took a deep breath of the crisp, night air, I thought to myself, *This is it, this is the last time you look back at your past.*

I turned back to take one last look at where I used to work; the warehouse which housed all my old pains for years and years, the latter now burnt to ash.

Then, I turned back toward the road and began walking away, not looking back, but only looking forward for something new.

Time to start fresh in a new, better place.

Author's Notes

I'm so thankful to be given an opportunity to be able to print my book. It truly is a dream come true. I've worked on this for 5 months and it was amazing to complete it. It took a lot of out me mentally and emotionally, opening up old wounds and putting myself in a dark place to write these out to the best of my ability.

Hope you enjoyed it, or at least felt something from it. That's my intention writing these poetry collections - to incite a reaction and hope what I'm going through struck a chord with any of you.

Writing was my creative outlet, and this collection was me going through the motions and acceptance of my scars and what makes me so messed up.

I want to give a hearty thank you to friends and loved ones for encouraging me to write this to completion, ensuring I don't fall too deep into self-inflicted depression when writing this, and being the first few to want to buy this. You know who you are.

I also want to thank my parents and family members. You gave me the inspiration and material needed to write this book. You also pushed me to want to make it as good as I can.

I want to thank my printing manager for being so patient with me with making the physical editions excellent, and something I can be proud of.

Last but definitely not least, I want to thank you, dear reader. Thank you for reading a rather vulnerable part of my life. Here's to hoping you open up all that's defective about you and accept it as part of who you are. Learn to not let that control you and seek help if you do need it. You're not alone, you never are alone.

Other works from **DJ Productions**

Rainclouds